To: Jill

From Amy

The
PERFECT
Friend

CHRIS SHEA

Published by J. Countryman, a division of Thomas Nelson, Inc, Nashville, Tennessee 37214.

Project manager—Terri Gibbs.

Designed by UDG|DesignWorks, Sisters, Oregon.

ISBN 1-4041-0181-0

http://www.thomasnelson.com
http://www.jcountryman.com

Printed and bound in the United States of America

To Kim Shea

Everyone should be so blessed
to have a daughter
like you.

There is perfection
in a tiny shell lying on
the shore,

and perfection echoes
in the notes

of songbirds on the
windowsill.

Perfection sparkles in the
starlight

of a moonless
winter sky,

and whenever I picture the
perfect friend,

you are the one
who comes
to mind.

Yours is the voice
I long to hear

calling on the phone,

yours the face
I love to see

standing at the door,

because you always bring
such happiness

everywhere you
go.

You are the best
a friend could
be,

and a smile would never
leave your face

So
— Beautiful

so
thoughtful

so
kind

you're
making
me blush!

if you heard what's often
said of you.

Just by being you,

You beautify the
world.

(If you were a flower
        at the nursery

they would always be
out of you.)

You understand my
feelings

I
understand.

and treat them with
such care,

I often wonder where
you came from.

(Heaven always comes
to mind.)

For every time you've
given me

an extra little push,

or lifted me up

when I was feeling down,

or made me laugh

when I was
feeling blue,

endless

gratitude.

Thank you

for being my friend,

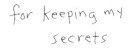

for keeping my
secrets

and believing

I really
can
do it!!

in
my
dreams.

I will always be
grateful our first
"hello"

became a
" come on in ! "

With just the perfect
blend of
" you ? "
" me, too ! "

our friendship was
begun....

There is perfection
in a tiny hand
that gathers seashells
on the
shore,

and perfection in a little ear

that hears the
songbirds sing.

Perfection sparkles
in the eyes

of campers beneath
a moonless sky,

and as long as I live
it will always be true
   that whenever I picture
         the perfect friend,

that friend
will always
be
you.